Now Are Ye the Sons of GOD

D. G. Hanscomb

Ideas into Books®
WESTVIEW
Kingston Springs, Tennessee

Ideas into Books®
W E S T V I E W
P.O. Box 605
Kingston Springs, TN 37082
www.publishedbywestview.com

ISBN 978-1-62880-095-1

Second edition, August 2016

Good faith efforts have been made to trace copyrights on materials
    included in this publication. If any copyrighted material has
    been included without permission and due acknowledgment,
    proper credit will be inserted in future printings after notice has
    been received.

Printed in the United States of America on acid free paper.

Dedication

It is with much pleasure that I have chosen to dedicate this book to Sister Lillian K. Buquo (Lewis). She is the mother of the most treasured woman in my life, my best friend and wife of over forty years, Sister Mary F. Hanscomb (Buquo).

Sister Buquo is a Holy Ghost filled woman and a truly dedicated mother in Zion. An individual ministering to others with her benevolent deeds while at the same time reaching out to those who may not know God in the power of His resurrection.

She has encouraged so many individuals in so many different ways in a very positive manner over the past six decades of her living for the Lord in the beauty of Holiness.

D. G. Hanscomb

Contents

Chapter One: Sons of God–Sons of Man

In this letter I shall strive diligently to differentiate between the **Sons of Man** and the **Sons of God**. To have a better understanding of the many moves of God's Spirit in this world's history we must acknowledge how mortal man has repeatedly interrupted them. We will witness the challenged Will of God by the very souls that He alone created.

Before reaching out for a better understanding of the monotheistic God of Abraham, His church, and His doctrine from a humbled place, let our personal lives be transparent before Him as we seek spiritual direction from the Divine.

As the annals of history are cracked open for the world to see, let us view our "Pure Apostolic Heritage" from a serious academic perspective.

> "For as many as are led by the Spirit of God, they are the **Sons of God**."

> Romans 8:14

1

Who then are the **Sons of God** and who are the **Sons of Man**? To qualify to be a **Son of God** one must be born of the Spirit of God. When God said, "Let us make man" in Genesis 1:26, He was not talking to Himself and was certainly not talking to another identity in His Godhead. He was actually talking to the **Sons of God** whom He sired before the foundation of the world, the angels.

> "And God said, Let us make man in our image, after our likeness."

> Genesis 1:26

The innumerable angels were the **Sons of God** because they were created by the Spirit of God. When God created the angels before the foundation of the world, He automatically became the Heavenly Father. He was the "Father Almighty" or the Alpha and the Omega. This is exactly why Jesus could tell John on the Isle of Patmos that He was the Alpha and that He alone was the Omega.

> "I am Alpha and Omega, the beginning and the end, the first and the last."

> Revelation 22:13

2

When Jesus told the Jews of His day in John 8:58, "before Abraham was I am," He chose to refer to Abraham because the Jews were referring to their father Abraham. Jesus could have said just as well, "before the angels were I am," because He was the Almighty Father Incarnate who knows no beginning.

Now the Father Almighty must not be confused with His first manifestation as the Father of Creation because He was already the Father Almighty.

In eternity we understand that God has no starting point to build upon. When Moses wrote "In the beginning God" in Genesis 1:1, he was writing as a mortal individual knowing about beginnings.

Therefore, the terminologies "beginning" and "ending" are totally consumed by God because He cannot relate to either of them. When we speak of the Father Almighty that existed before all things we are speaking of the Alpha and the Omega, who became God Incarnate in Christ the Messiah. There were three manifestations of Almighty God in three different dispensations of mortal time. The three manifestations of the God of Abraham were:

The Father Almighty as:
1) The Father of Creation
2) The Son of Redemption
3) The Holy Ghost in us

The Father of Creation was God Almighty; the Son of Redemption was God Almighty; and the Holy Ghost is God Almighty.

Tertullian (155-220 A.D.) was the first Latin writer in the church to use the terms person and substance in his description of the Godhead. From that time in history, those words were erroneously applied to the nature of God by some theologians of that day.

When one talks about persons, we refer to individuals. There are not three separate individuals within the nature of the God of Abraham. Neither are there three Gods as was believed by Joseph Smith, the founder of the Mormon Church. Jehovah is God and knows no other gods. The Apostle John writes about the activities of Almighty God.

> "For there are three that bear record in heaven, the Father, the Word, and the Holy Ghost: and these three are one."

> I John 5:7

4

John was not implying that there were three Gods or three separate identities communicating in heaven. He was referring to the three separate activities of Almighty God that are recorded there. The Father of creation, the Son of redemption (the Word or Logos) and the Holy Ghost.

In the first century church, many of those saints who experienced the New Birth lived in all three dispensations of God's timetable. They were Jews before the birth of the Messiah and knew God as the Father of creation. They came to know Jesus as their Redeemer and experienced the infilling of the Holy Ghost on the day of Pentecost but always saw Jesus as the Father Almighty incarnate...the Immanuel.

An Israeli prisoner in modern history unearthed the edge of an elaborate mosaic (piece of artwork) on the floor of what is believed to be one of the oldest Apostolic Churches on Earth.

Archaeologists have dated this particular church in the Holy Land back to the third century A.D., decades before Christianity was made the official religion of the previously pagan Roman Empire in the fourth century by Emperor Constantine the Great.

The mosaic includes drawings of fish, which were an ancient symbol of Christianity predating the widespread use of the cross. An inscription in this piece of artwork mentions an Apostolic woman who donated an altar of prayer to the church. The dedication on the flooring reveals the words, "To God Jesus Christ."

This God Almighty was the Alpha and Omega, God Incarnate in Christ and God Incarnate in us through the baptism of the Holy Ghost.

> "To whom God would make known what is the riches of the glory of this mystery among the Gentiles; which is Christ in you, the hope of glory: Whom we preach, warning every man, and teaching every man in all wisdom; that we may present every man perfect in Christ Jesus."

> Colossians 1:27-28

The first time that I was in an Apostolic Church, God gave me the revelation of His Incarnation. In the Book of Isaiah, we witness a very clear and distinct dialogue between God and His prophet. The Lord was very adamant about

His identity and chose to remove any doubt concerning His Sovereignty by adding titles to His saving Name.

> "For unto us a child is born, unto us a son is given: and the government shall be upon his shoulder; and his name shall be called Wonderful, Counsellor, The Mighty God, The Everlasting Father, The Prince of Peace."

> Isaiah 9:6

To the **Sons of God** who were born of the Spirit of God in the first century church, Jesus was known as follows:

- ❖ Jesus the Wonderful
- ❖ Jesus the Counsellor
- ❖ Jesus the Mighty God
- ❖ Jesus the **Everlasting Father**
- ❖ Jesus the Prince of Peace

Why would the Lord instruct Isaiah to prophesy that the child would be referred to as the Everlasting Father if He was not indeed the Almighty Father Incarnate or the Alpha and Omega?

The angels were the **Sons of God** being created by the Spirit of God. One day, when God asked Job where he was when the universe was being formed and the angels, the **Sons of God**, shouted. To understand the Godhead one must go beyond the beginning because God has no beginning.

> "Where was thou when I laid the foundations of the earth? Declare if thou hast understanding. Who hath laid the measures thereof, if thou knowest? Or who hath stretched the line upon it? Whereupon are the foundations thereof fastened? Or who laid the cornerstone thereof; When the morning stars sang together, and all the **Sons of God** shouted for joy?"

> Job 38:4-7

Adam, the first human being, was a **Son of God** because he was born not of flesh and blood but by the Spirit of God.

> "Which was the son of Enos, which was the son of Seth, which was the son of Adam, which was the **Son of God**."

> Luke 3:38

8

All men after Adam and Eve are referred to in the Bible as the **Sons of Man** because they were born of the flesh and not of the Spirit of God.

When I was in the Catholic Church, I was taught and did teach that there are two categories of sin: the mortal sins and the venial sins. However, with God there are no big sins and there are no small sins. There is really only one sin that we can commit and that is the sin of disobedience to God. Where was the sin in the beautiful Garden of Eden? Was it in eating the forbidden fruit, or was it in disobeying the voice of God? If Adam and Eve had obeyed the Lord they would have never eaten the forbidden fruit. If Israel had obeyed the Lord, they could have saved Moses a trip up the mountain to secure the Lord's commandments.

> "And they heard the voice of the Lord God walking in the garden in the cool of the day: and Adam and his wife hid themselves from the presence of the Lord God amongst the trees of the garden. And the Lord God called unto Adam, and said unto him, where art thou?"

> Genesis 3:8-9

9

We are born the **Sons of Man** by nature and have because of the cross of Calvary the ability to become the **Sons of God** by divine intervention through the New Birth.

One third of the **Sons of God** in heaven were kicked out of heaven as were the **Sons of God** kicked out of the beautiful garden of Eden that the Lord had personally prepared for them.

Jesus Christ was referred to as both the **Son of God** and the **Son of Man** because He was born of the mortal woman Mary and of the Spirit of God. He was indeed human as well as Divine.

> "And the angel answered and said unto her, The Holy Ghost shall come upon thee, and the power of the Highest shall overshadow thee: therefore also that holy thing which shall be born of thee shall be called the **Son of God**."

> Luke 1:35

Regarding the Godhead, one must be able to differentiate between when Jesus spoke as a man and when He spoke as the Almighty Father.

> "When Jesus came into the coasts of Caesarea Philippi, he asked his disciples, saying, Whom

do men say that I the **Son of Man** am?"

Matthew 16:13

God's plan for our salvation is all about being Born Again not of the flesh but by the Spirit of God that makes us the **Sons of God**. I was Roman Catholic and this is not an attack on Catholicism. This is an attack on *man-made* religious Christianity no matter what name it comes under.

> "But as many as received him, to them gave he power to become the **Sons of God,** even to them that believe on his name: which were born not of blood, nor of the will of the flesh, nor of the will of man, but of God."

John 1:12-13

It is imperative that we understand that the Word of God the Holy Bible was written by the **Sons of God** who were born again of the water and of the Spirit of God. The Word of God must therefore be interpreted by the **Sons of God** who experienced the new birth. It is all about being Born Again!

Apostolic people believe that the Holy Bible is the inspired Word of God, holy, true and

11

unadulterated. The **Sons of Man** therefore have no inherent right to properly interpret the Word of God.

The name over your church door will not save you. It is the process of being born again that will save you. In the beginning it was simply His church and His doctrine with the saints enjoying their Pentecostal experience.

When God visited mankind, He came with the intention of making lost children His sons and His daughters through the New Birth. In doing so, although we were created a little lower than the angels, one day on the other side we who have been born again of God's Spirit will become equal with the angels.

> "Thou madest him a little lower than the angels; thou crownedest him with glory and honour, and didst set him over the works of thy hands."

> Hebrews 2:7

When one experiences the New Birth they become new creatures in Christ Jesus. The Bible says in 11 Corinthians 5:17 that old things pass away and all things become new.

> "Neither can they die any
> more: for they are equal unto the
> angels; and are the children of God,
> being the children of the
> resurrection."

Luke 20:36

To become a Christian or follower of Christ the New Birth is not optional; neither is it negotiable. If we choose to be Apostolic, there must be nothing about us that is not Apostolic. We must be willing to meticulously lay our lives on the altar with the same love and compassion as He laid Himself on the cross.

The true verdict of history is not what *man-made* religious Christianity has presented to humanity, but what God has sealed, charming the heavens with reverberating echoes of absolute truth.

Truth has stood the test of time and will forever stand. Therefore, it is by far better to remain with a flawed alliance than to risk the uncertain consequences of breaking from it.

Holiness is like prophecy. It does not start with mortals. It does not start on the inside of a human being and it does not start on the outside of one. When God becomes incarnate within these walls of flesh through the baptism of the Holy Spirit, we become heirs of holiness, which is an attribute of God Himself. When the Lord fills us with this power, it takes us to a whole new level.

Holiness is not to be seen as a burdensome yoke that we somehow inherited at an altar of repentance, but as an attribute of God within, which becomes part of our identity. This landmark in our lives not only identifies with the new creature that we become, but with God Himself, who is holy.

Martin Luther, the sixteenth century reformer who was previously an Augustinian monk in the Roman Catholic Church, wrote in the third of his 95 Theses to Pope Leo X that:

> "Yet it does not mean inward repentance only, as there is no inward repentance that does not manifest itself outwardly through various mortifications of the flesh."

It is absolutely imperative that absolute truth be emphatically spoken in this controversial world of *man-made* religious Christianity. A temple without God's presence is not God's temple!

Basilicas and cathedrals that stand as monuments fit for royalty can soar to the heavens

14

but will be simply hollow buildings if the king is not in residence. So it is with human temples, male or female, most of which are dedicated to other gods.

The *man-made* Christian church that found birth in the fertile ground of the fourth century after Emperor Theodosus I made the trinity doctrine civil law in the Roman Empire was simply the union (once again) between political influence and Apostolic compromise.

This church is fated to cease in the midnight hour driving their leaders into silence while the Pure Apostolic Church that has been led and is being led by the anointed **Sons of God** is destined to total victory—His candid church.

If anyone anywhere wants to identify with the first century church or the Pure Apostolic Church, they must prepare themselves to identify also with the teachings of the first century church. If the Pontiff in Rome was the true successor of Peter, would he not be teaching exactly what Peter taught? To be a true successor of Peter, one must be a **Son of God** that personally experienced the New Birth.

There is only one church that has transforming power to make us the **Sons of God** and there is only one doctrine to become partakers of that church.

> "And I say also unto thee, that thou are Peter, and upon this rock I will build MY CHURCH; and the gates of hell shall not prevail against it."

> Matthew 16:18

It must be emphatically stated that this church was to be HIS church and the doctrine of this church would be HIS doctrine.

> "But though we, or an angel from heaven, preach any other gospel unto you than that which we have preached unto you, let him be accursed.

> As we said before, so say I now again, If any man preach any other gospel unto you than that ye have received, let him be accursed."

> Galatians 1:8-9

The universal church that was tailored to meet the needs of "whosoever will" is God's glorious church that was undivided and is still undivided.

This church was entrusted to the **Sons of God** by Christ Himself on the Day of Pentecost or the "Feast of the First Fruits." It is the same singular church spoken of in the Book of Ephesians that will be presented to the Lord by Himself.

> "That He might present it to himself a glorious church, not having spot, or wrinkle, or any such thing; but that it should be holy and without blemish."

> Ephesians 5:27

Therefore no one has the inherent right to claim ownership of the church that was purchased at a great price. The church belongs to Him and to Him alone. We do not have a monopoly on His blood-washed church! Anyone, anywhere can become a **Son of God** if they simply obey God's plan for their soul's salvation.

> "There is one body, and one Spirit, even as ye are called in one hope of your calling; One Lord, one faith, one baptism, One God and Father of all who is above all, and through all, and in you all."

> Ephesians 4:4-6

Apostolic Pentecostals rejecting denominationalism that was never in the mind of God, were from the beginning. We are Apostolic because we live, believe, and teach the Apostles' doctrine. We are Pentecostal because we have experienced the baptism of the Holy Ghost, which was the driving force behind the Apostles in the days of the early church. It was and is the fuel upon which the powerful Apostolic zeal operates.

We are living in a day where there are different churches seemingly on every corner, each one claiming to be right while to them the others are wrong. To say that they are right and that the others are wrong immediately puts both churches on the defensive.

Apostolic people have never in the history of the church said that we are right and that others are wrong. God's church has nothing to prove to anyone! What we do say, however, is that what the Messiah passed down to the Apostles is right and everything outside of "Thus sayeth the Lord" is wrong. Those people through the many centuries of time that have added to and taken away from the Word of God have already toyed with the author. The ecumenical councils have always been about addition and omission.

I would never go to an exclusive Italian restaurant and ask for chop-sticks. Neither would I go to *man-made* religious Christianity and ask for truth.

It is not the creeds, ecumenical councils, theologies, philosophies, or one's thesis that will save people. Hungry hearts must get back to the "Word of the Lord" that transforms us. God did not write the creeds nor did He call ecumenical councils. That is the work of *man-made* religious Christianity. If the Lord wanted to change things, He would have inspired men to re-write the Bible. If the Apostles were the authors of the Apostles Creed, would it not have been recorded in the Bible as were their other writings? The first mention of the Apostles Creed was by Bishop Ambros of Milan, Italy, in the fourth century. It was in that century that Emperor Constantine I wrote the "Edit of Milam."

> "For I testify unto every man that heareth the words of the prophecy of this book, If any man shall add unto these things, God shall add unto him the plagues that are written in this book. And if any man shall take away from the words of the book of this prophecy, God shall take away his part out of

> the book of life, and out of the holy
> city, and from the things which are
> written in this book."

Revelation 22:18-19

We will see as time goes on that the Christian Church has been divided for almost two thousand years and remains divided.

The Apostolic Church promoting the monotheistic nature of the God of Abraham being led by the **Sons of God** that experienced the New Birth and the *man-made* church that has been led and is still being led by the **Sons of Man** that have never experienced the New Birth.

If it took the power of the Holy Ghost to inspire men to speak and to write the Word of God, is it not logical that it will take the same influence to inspire men to understand the Word of God?

Christianity is all about having a relationship with God Himself. Although the creeds and ecumenical councils through the ages have some literary credibility, they as the books of the Apocrypha in the intertestamental period cannot compare with the Anointed Word of God. At the end of the day, the only thing that is going to matter is the TRUTH and the truth is found in the Word of God.

The Messiah instructed a **Son of Man** concerning His plan for salvation. The man's name was Nicademous, who was actually a son within Judaism. Jesus personally offered this Jewish leader an opportunity to become a **Son of God** in saying, "Ye must be born again." Christianity is all about being born of the Spirit of God which makes us the **Sons of God**.

> "Jesus answered, 'Verily, verily, I say unto thee, except a man be born of water and of the Spirit, he CANNOT enter into the kingdom of God." [I didn't say it. Jesus said it.] That which is born of the flesh is flesh; and that which is born of the Spirit is Spirit."

> John 3:5-6

Let's get back to the first century church! The Lord instructed His disciples not to leave the city of Jerusalem until they became endowed with power from heaven. The one hundred and twenty human beings including the mother of Jesus were about to experience the New Birth which would transform their lives forever into the **Sons of God**.

> "And when the day of Pentecost was fully come, they

were all with one accord in one place. And suddenly, there came a sound from heaven as of a rushing mighty wind, and it filled all the house where they were sitting. And there appeared unto them cloven tongues like as of fire, and it sat upon each of them. And they were all filled with the Holy Ghost and began to speak with other tongues, as the Spirit gave them utterance."

Acts 2:1-4

The people in Jerusalem immediately saw an amazing change in those individuals who were experiencing the unparalleled power of God on that special day. The Apostle Paul explains how the experience changed his life forever. He became a new creature in Christ Jesus.

"For in Christ Jesus neither circumcision availeth anything, nor uncircumcision, but a new creature."

Galatians 6:15

Paul not only experienced an amazing change in his life, but had a new understanding of what a real Jew should be after the New Birth experience.

> "For he is NOT a Jew, which
> is one outwardly; neither is that
> circumcision, which is outward in
> the flesh: But he IS a Jew, which is
> one inwardly; and circumcision is
> that of the heart, in the Spirit, and
> not in the letter; whose praise is not
> of men, but of God."

> Romans 2:28-29

One does not have to change when there is no change required. If we choose to lean on our own understanding and tailor a private interpretation of the Word of God, we automatically become members of *man-made* religious Christianity. The words of Solomon the son of King David and Bathsheba should ring loud and clear in the ears of those individuals who sincerely seek His will for their lives.

> "Trust in the Lord with all
> thine heart: and lean not unto thine
> own understanding. In all thy ways,
> acknowledge him, and he shall
> direct thy paths."

> Proverbs 3:5-6

Being witness to the baptism of the Holy Ghost many were pricked in their hearts realizing what they had actually done, while others mocked. Some of the Jews went as far as to say that they were drunk.

> "But Peter, standing up with the eleven, lifted up his voice, and said unto them, Ye men of Judaea, and all ye that dwell at Jerusalem, be this known unto you, and hearken to my words: For these are not drunken, as ye suppose, seeing it is but the third hour of the day. But this is that which was spoken by the prophet Joel: And it shall come to pass in the last days, sayeth God, I will pour out of my Spirit upon all flesh: and your sons and your daughters shall prophesy, and your young men shall see visions, and your old men shall dream dreams."

Acts 2:14-17

When they were witnessing this amazing event, they did not know that the Messiah had given Peter the keys to the kingdom of God. They would have asked Peter to give them the keys instead of asking the group what they should do if they had known of this transition.

"Now when they heard this, they were pricked in their heart, and said unto Peter and to the rest of the Apostles, Men and brethren, what shall we do? Then Peter said unto them, REPENT and be BAPTIZED every one of you in the NAME of Jesus Christ for the remission of sins, and ye shall receive the gift of the HOLY GHOST. [The message has not changed and is very much relevant today.] For the promise is unto you, and to your children, and to all that are afar off, even as many as the Lord our God shall call. And with many other words did he testify and exhort, saying, Save yourselves from this untoward generation. Then they that gladly received his word were baptized: and the same day there were added unto them about three thousand souls."

Acts 2:37-41

After God fills us with the Holy Ghost, we automatically become the **Sons of God** because He takes up residence and becomes Incarnate in us. He then can speak through the **Sons of God**

25

because He is in us. His ministers are the anointed **Sons of God**.

God not only becomes Incarnate in us, but His attributes as well become Incarnate in us. It becomes love Incarnate, peace Incarnate, joy Incarnate, the way Incarnate and truth Incarnate. When an individual becomes a **Son of God** they take on the attributes of their Heavenly Father.

To those who receive the revelation of who Jesus really is through the Word of God become the **Sons of God** through obedience to His Word.

> "Beloved, now are we the **Sons of God** and it doth not yet appear what we shall be: but we know that when He shall appear, we shall be like Him; for we shall see Him as He is."

> 1 John 3:2

Without the New Birth, people have only *man-made* religious Christianity and their conscience to lean upon.

> "Ever learning, and never able to come to the knowledge of the truth."

> 11 Timothy 3:7

In this the end-time, we must soberly take a good look at what is freedom and what is actually bondage. The churches that reject the doctrine of the Apostles, no matter what name appears on their banners, is simply in religious bondage.

When someone experiences the New Birth, there is a change, a spark of life that every young Christian experiences. So what happens when we are saved? Our human spirit is brought to life and the human spirit is literally Born Again as the Spirit of God brings the human spirit to life and takes up residence. Once that happens, we have Divine revelation inside of us. Suddenly our human condition and what God did in the God-Man Jesus Christ makes sense. Before we did not understand His Word and now we do. We find ourselves drawn to Him, thankful to Him and in love with Him.

> "God is a Spirit: and they that worship him must worship Him in Spirit and in truth."

> John 4:24

This is the foundation of the Christian life. It isn't about doctrines, teachings, acting a certain way, or going to church or Sunday school. It is about having a relationship with God! It isn't about learning, studying, thinking, or meditating. It is about touching God with your human spirit. To the recipient salvation becomes very personal.

I have found that understanding spiritual things does not come from reading, or thinking about God. Neither does it come from exercising your will and demanding to know about Him, nor opening your emotions to feel Him. You can't get to God by following a formula or a form, by going to church, or to a holy man. There are no intermediaries! One understands God when He reveals Himself to you! Man is made up of a body, soul, and spirit. Only the human spirit can comprehend God. Being a good human being does not qualify us as being Christian. There are good people in this world that have never heard of God.

God's will is that we search within our own spirits, exploring and executing innate potential, while identifying with the self as well as the Divine.

No other animal was made in His image— only man! But proud and arrogant man tries to fill that God-shaped void with everything but God— knowledge, possessions, pleasures, etc. Instead we try to create God in our image. We sense that there might be a Supreme Being up there, so we make God into what we think that He should be or what we would like for Him to be. Man worships the sun, the moon, the elements, teachings, and doctrines.

I have found unless we accept God's plan for our lives and have our human spirit made alive, we have only our vain imagination and perhaps religion (*man-made* religious Christianity) that is led by the **Sons of Man** but not true revelation.

Christianity is about relationship, not religion. Religion is simply doing things, trying to be good, and living up to a standard. True Christianity is about having a relationship with God and literally letting Him change you one day at a time.

I have found that in Christianity it is not always what one agrees upon or disagrees upon, but what one allows themselves to do or does not allow themselves to do. To excel in the things of the Lord, which we all want to do, a person must humbly, honestly, and sincerely self-acknowledge their own spiritual identity.

In reality, a costume is put on to pretend to be a particular individual. When a person puts on a real uniform, it automatically becomes their identity!

For salvation, giving up the ways of the world is not optional. I personally feel that the real question is very simple: do I want the old man, or do I want the New Birth?

To understand what happened in the early church, one must get back to His undivided church. Prophetic scripture has cautioned that *man-made* religious Christianity which has been and continues to be led by the **Sons of Man** has been fated to cease in this the end-time. Christianity is all about being Born Again as it was in the beginning. God, His doctrine, and His love for humanity does not change.

When I was studying for the priesthood in the Roman Catholic Church, I had serious questions concerning my Catholic faith. Although I was indeed sincere in wanting to please God over the years, I had slowly become a victim of institutionalized *man-made* religious Christianity that is not led by the **Sons of God** but by the **Sons of Man**. I knew about the twenty-one ecumenical councils of the church and their creeds but as a Catholic I felt that there was something missing.

One of my questions to my professors was: Are we to believe that the creeds throughout history along with the ecumenical councils are more Orthodox than the Bible? For my proper answers the Lord of all the Lords had to take me back in time to His undivided church before people became indoctrinated by those **Sons of Man** who refused to accept the reality of becoming Born Again through the New Birth experience.

Let us compare a couple of events in history with the Holy Word of God and decide if those involved were being led by the **Sons of Man** or if they were being led by the **Sons of God**.

At the Council of Trent in the sixteenth century, church tradition was discussed at length. The Council was opened by Pope Paul III on December 13, 1545, and was closed by Pope Pius IV on December 4, 1563. The Council declared that church TRADITION and the Bible were equal valid sources of the Roman Catholic Church.

When the "repent" of Acts 2:38 is replaced with "penance," the Word of God is then superseded by church tradition. We know what was written at the Council of Trent. Now let us look at "Thus sayeth the Word of the Lord."

> "For laying aside the commandment of God, ye hold the TRADITION of men."

> Mark 7:8

The following scripture as was the previous scripture is found in your Bible that was written by the **Sons of God**.

31

> "Beware lest any man spoil you through Philosophy and vain deceit after the TRADITION of men, after the rudiments of the world, and not after Christ. For in HIM dwelleth all the fullness of the Godhead bodily."

> Colossians 2:8-9

Just because Pope Paul III and Pope Pius IV declared it, does not make it so!

Now let us look at the teaching of John Calvin who was a former Roman Catholic priest. He lived in the sixteenth century as well. He was totally against anyone who did not support the trinity doctrine and actually had Michael Servetus burned to death on October 27, 1553 because of it.

John Calvin, the founding father of the Presbyterian Church, was responsible for the teaching of the "Once saved always saved" doctrine.

We know the teaching of John Calvin; now let's look at "Thus sayeth the Word of the Lord" that was written by the **Sons of God**.

> "...Thus sayeth the Lord, Ye have forsaken me, and therefore have I also left you..."

> II Chronicles 12:5

32

I have a question for you. How could anyone expect to go to heaven when this life is over if they stop following Jesus Christ?

> "From that time, many of His disciples went back, and walked no more with Him."
>
> John 6:66

Is it possible to have a genuine walk with the Lord and eventually backslide? Absolutely! God will not be mocked by the souls that He alone created.

> "And he went out to meet Asa, and said unto him, Hear ye me, Asa, and all of Judah and Benjamin; The Lord is with you, while ye be with him; and if ye seek him, he will be found of you; but if ye forsake him, he WILL forsake you."
>
> II Chronicles 15:2

Just because John Calvin the **Son of Man** that formerly taught in the Roman Catholic Church said it, does not make it so!

It is high time that we seriously take another look at the Old Paths that are clearly outlined in the Word of God and once again walk in them.

Apostolic people are NOT the sons and daughters of *man-made* religious Christianity. Apostolic ministers who cherish their calling within the five-fold ministry are not the descendents of the ministers who embrace the traditions of men, neither are they the sons of Ishmael, but heirs of the prophet Isaac.

These two sons of Abraham have not stopped fighting and as we witness in modern times will not stop fighting until the Lord comes for His blood-washed church. I personally flew my family to New York City when the twin towers were destroyed by the radical sons of Ishmael. These individuals that started their venture of terror in Boston had absolutely no consideration for human life.

The Apostle Paul, writing to the Galatians, clearly points out our heritage as the sons of Isaac.

> "For it is written, that Abraham had two sons [Ishmael and Isaac] the one by a handmaid [Hagar], the other by a freewoman [Sarah]. But he who was of the bondwoman [Ishmael] was born after the flesh; but he of the freewoman [Isaac] was by promise. Which things are an allegory: for these are the two covenants; the

34

one from the Mount Sinai, which gendereth to bondage, which is Agar [Hagar]: For this Agar is Mount Sinai in Arabia, and answereth to Jerusalem which now is, and is in bondage with her children. But Jerusalem, which is above, is free, which is the mother of us all. Now we bretheren, as Isaaic was, are the Children Of Promise. But as then he that was born after the flesh [Ishmaelites] persecuted him [Jews] that was born after the Spirit, even so it is now. Nevertheless, what sayeth the scripture? Cast out the bondwoman, and her son; for the son of the bondwoman [Ishmael] shall not be heir with the son of the freewoman [Isaac]. So then bretheren, we are not children of the bondwoman, but of the free."

Galatians 4:22-26, 28-31

In Islam, they teach that Jesus was a prophet. We do not believe that. We believe that Jesus was the prophesied Messiah. He was Almighty God, The Alpha and Omega Incarnate.

In this portion of scripture, we witness a type and shadow of what appears in the modern world of Christianity: **The Sons of Man** and **The Sons of God**.

The Messiah talked openly about that "Living Water" that sets the captive free. We were all born in bondage, but those who accept the doctrine of the Apostles are free. They are free indeed!

Oh, that we that have been redeemed by the blood of the Lamb might open our spiritual ears as we hear the voice of the Master as it echoes throughout the hills of old Judeah.

To compromise God's Word is simply to lead us back to Rome. I have been to spiritual Rome, and I shall not allow the spirit of compromise to take me back.

There are very few people that sit on Apostolic church pews that have a self-righteous, better-than-thou attitude. However small their number, I have news for those individuals as well. They are not going to take me back to spiritual Rome, either. In the fall of 1972, I got my foot on the rock, my sails set, and my eyes on that city whose builder and whose maker is God.

Esau begrudgingly learned that when you feed the flesh you lose something more precious. You lose your birthright!

If a person steps out of the brightness of day into a very dark room, he finds himself momentarily blinded. However, the longer he stays in the room, the more visible things become. Perhaps he sees the outline of a table or perhaps a shelf on the wall. Be not deceived and be advised that he has not seen the light, but has gotten used to the darkness.

Those who have willingly chosen to compromise Apostolic Theology and their standards of Holiness that are clearly outlined in the Word of God say that we are in bondage and that they have actually seen the light. Again, Saints of God, be not deceived in this midnight hour. They have not seen the light as they claim, but because of their compromising spirit, they themselves have gotten used to the darkness.

> "Now as Jannes and Jambres with-stood Moses, so do these also resist the TRUTH: men of corrupt minds, reprobate concerning the faith."
>
> II Timothy 3:8

I guess the real question is this: What do I want for myself and those that I love in this life? Do I want *man-made* religious Christianity that was designed and tailored by men to meet the needs of the flesh, or do I want "Pure Apostolic" power that was experienced and has been experienced from the beginning of His church? Saints, at the end of the day, the only thing that is going to really matter is the truth. Oh! that the church of the living God once again tap into the immeasurable power of prayer.

> "Then said Jesus to those Jews which believed on him, If ye continue in my word, then are ye my disciples indeed; And ye shall know the TRUTH, and the truth shall make you free."

> John 8:31-32

When I was in the Catholic faith, one of our Archbishops, Robert E. Lucey of San Antonio, Texas, said that the authority in the Roman Catholic Church was obviously and openly heretical. The Vatican did not appreciate his publicized comment and after being petitioned to do so by the priests he supervised, ordered him to retire. This influential Archbishop died on August 1, 1977. Catholic people do not need to wait for word that this bishop was canonized. It is not going to happen!

The morning that I found myself sitting in an Apostolic Church was the very morning that I was on my way to St. Thomas Aquinas Roman Catholic Church.

Following is one of the Summa Theologica of Aquinas concerning the treatment of heretics. Thomas Aquinas wrote:

> "With regard to heretics, two points must be observed: one on their own side; the other, on the side of the church. On their own side there is the sin, whereby they deserve not only to be separated from the church by excommunication, but also to be severed from the world by DEATH. For it is a much graver matter to corrupt the faith which quickens the soul, than to forge money, which supports temporal life. Wherefore if forgers of money and other evil doers are forthwith condemned to death by the secular authority, much more reason is there for heretics, as soon as they are

convicted of heresy, to be not only excommunicated but even put to DEATH. On the part of the church, however, there is mercy with looks to the conversion of the wanderer, wherefore she condemns not at once, but after the first and second admonitions as the Apostle directs: after that, if he is yet stubborn, the church no longer hoping for his conversion, looks to the salvation of others, by excommunicating him and separating him from the church, and furthermore delivers him to the secular tribunal to be exterminated thereby from the world by DEATH." [There was no separation of church and state in the thirteenth century.]

Summa, 11-11, A-11, Art. 3

"Thou shalt not kill" is one of the ten commandments that the Pure Apostolic Church that is led by the **Sons of God** practices on a daily basis. We do NOT kill people.

St. Thomas Aquinas lived in the thirteenth century and belonged to the Dominican Order. This Catholic priest is held in his church to be the model teacher for those studying for the priesthood—the master and patron of Roman Catholic schools. At the Second Vatican Council, Pope Paul VI referred to him as "The Angelic Doctor."

John Greenwood was imprisoned and on April 6, 1593, was hanged in England for his teaching of "Separation of Church and State." There had not been any separation of church and state since the days of Constantine I in the fourth century. This stigma lasted well up into the eighteenth century when President James Madison of the United States asked for a "Wall of Separation" between the two.

Is this in the Holy Bible being part of the Pure Apostolic Church that was and is being led by the **Sons of God** or is this part of *man-made* religious Christianity that has been and is being led today by the **Sons of Man**? Is this really important? When the angel of the Lord puts one foot on the land and one foot on the sea and declares time to be no more, this will be most important!

Chapter Two: The Trinity Doctrine

Who is the monotheistic God of Abraham that the sons of Judaism readily refer to as Yahweh and who is this Lord that the Apostolics often call upon as being the one and only Potentate that alone monitors the heavens and the earth?

Be advised that it is not God or the **Sons of God** who so often experience confusion and blurred visions of this identity. It is the **Sons of Man** as I was that experience the confusion in understanding the Lord's identity.

Luke was a learned individual and was remarkably knowledgeable concerning the Old Testament characters and their inspired writings. He said that Moses who is accredited for the writings of the first five books of the Holy Bible, referred to the Lord as being the God of Abraham.

"Now that the dead are raised
even Moses shewed at the bush
when he calleth the LORD the God

of Abraham, and the God of Isaac,
and the God of Jacob."

Luke 20:37

In this modern day of technology, the question concerning the God of Abraham and the Lord not only deserve an educated answer, but demands one. Just how many LORDS are there existing in the heavens above and in the earth below? Do the scriptures imply three Lords, or is there only one LORD?

The Apostle Paul is considered by historians to be one of the most significant figures of the Apostolic Age. He was indeed an intellectual having studied under the noted rabbi Gamaliel. He explained to the Ephesians that there is but one LORD!

"There is one body, and one Spirit, even as ye are called in one hope of your calling; ONE Lord, one faith, one baptism, One God and FATHER of all, who is above all, and through all, and in you all."

Ephesians 4:4-6

Now we know that there is but ONE Lord and that the FATHER is in us through the baptism of fire as it was experienced in the beginning on the

44

day of Pentecost. This one LORD apparently felt a need to reveal to humanity the so much debated mystery among the Gentiles:

> "To whom God would make known what is the riches of the glory of this mystery among the Gentiles; which is CHRIST in you, the hope of glory."

> Colossians 1:27

The Holy and unadulterated Word of God just informed us that the FATHER and JESUS were both in us. Brace yourself, there is a third on the way!

> "I indeed baptize you with water unto repentance: but he that cometh after me is mightier than I, whose shoes I am not worthy to bear! He shall baptize you with the HOLY GHOST, and with fire."

> Matthew 3:11

One more time, a qualified and worthy question demands, expects, and deserves, an educated response!

The Bible just revealed to us that the FATHER, the SON, and the HOLY GHOST are all in us. Our human bodies of clay were purposely designed by God as temples to house the Spirit of the Almighty. Are there three separate and distinct identities in these temples of clay, or is it the Lord God Almighty in His entirety that has taken up residence, who beforehand manifested Himself in three distinct and separate dispensations of time? Is it one single identity, or is it three separate identities living in our temples of clay?

> "Know yet not that ye are the
> temple of God, and *that* the Spirit
> of God dwelleth in you?"

> I Corinthians 3:16

Almighty God was LORD and created all things that are in heaven above and the things that are under the heavens here below. Almighty God was LORD Incarnate as he humbly walked the shores of Galilee among us and Almighty God is the LORD in us the hope of glory!

Not three Gods but one God; not three Almighties, but one Almighty; not three Lords, but one Lord!

As Jesus' Name Apostolic people, we must not only understand the threat but the seriousness of blatant heresies. The **Sons of Men** who have literally

46

chained themselves to spiritual darkness through their ritualisms and their formalities have no inherited right to properly interpret the Word of God, seeing that they throughout the church's history are not, neither have they been, led by the Spirit of God. Their promoting of *man-made* theologies, philosophies, ideologies, and personal theses simply amounts to spiritual adultery within Christendom if they are not in line with the Word of God.

One can neither divide or properly interpret the true meaning of being Born Again for themselves or for anyone else if they have not been subject to the unparalleled power of God and saved according to Biblical standards.

The 21 ecumenical councils have literally re-written the Bible. One can write all the creeds that they desire to write and call all the councils that they so desire, but at the end of the day, it is still "Thus sayeth the Word of the Lord." When the mortal puts on immortality and we stand before God, there must not be any question concerning our identity. We must present ourselves as being the **Sons of God**, not the **Sons of Man** that have not experienced this wonderful New Birth experience.

"This people draweth nigh unto
me with their mouth, and honoureth

> me with their lips; but their heart is far from me. But in vain they do worship me, teaching for doctrines the commandments of men."

Matthew 15:8-9

Oneness believers often gave their lives to stand against heresies entering into the church. This message of undying truth, accompanied with total devotion to our monotheistic God, was most notably displayed in the life and death of the Oneness martyr Michael Servetus.

Michael Servetus was a Spanish physician and theologian. He was born in Tadela, Spain, in the sixteenth century and studied medicine in Paris, France. Civil and church leaders condemned Servetus for not conforming, in his writings, to the widely accepted doctrine of trinitarianism.

In the writings of this man, we encounter his obvious stance concerning the trinity doctrine when he says it is an invention of the devil, an infernal falsity for the destruction of all Christianity.

Satan saw destruction within the Pure Apostolic Church as this consuming seed fell from his hand, only to find a firm lodging place in fertile ground. Was the cry of Servetus as they tied him to a stake to be burned alive a warning to those of us who would succeed him? Should we see the teaching of the trinity that descended upon the universal church in the second century as a spirit that came from wickedly controlled places? Has this doctrine of Tertullian been taken too lightly—even ignored—by some within Christendom? What is the true identity of the trinity doctrine?

Michael Servetus contended that even such able innovators as Martin Luther, the former Augustinian monk, and John Calvin, the former Roman Catholic priest, were not revolutionary enough, for they had not broken away from the dogma of the trinity.

Michael Servetus may well be regarded as one of the most outstanding figures of the early Reformation period. Pope Julius III, the well known hebephiliac (entangled in a love for boys) demanded the death of this Oneness theologian.

If Pope Julius III had been a real **Son of God** and a successor to the Apostle Peter, would he have been hanging out with young boys or demanding the death of the Oneness martyr Michael Servetus? The truth of the matter is that he was NOT a **Son of God**, but on the contrary, a **Son of Man** catering to the lusts of his own flesh.

49

The Catholic Church's involvement in continuing turmoil could not be overlooked. Pope Adrian VI, who was pope from 1522 until his death the next year, described the condition of the Catholic Church and the carnal activity surrounding the Vatican when he said he acknowledged that God permits persecution of the church on account of the sin of men, and especially of prelates and clergy. He knew well that for many years things deserving of abhorrence had gathered around the Holy See, sacred things have been misused, ordinances transgressed, so that in everything there had been a change for the worse.

Martin Luther, seen by many throughout history as a great reformer, was actually a **Son of Man**.

This former Augustinian monk would not convert to Judaism with their Oneness convictions and the Jews would not convert to his trinity doctrine. Being spurred by a spirit of hatred, Martin Luther chose to eliminate them all. In our day, it would been seen as harboring the spirit of ethnic-cleansing.

In 1543, Luther published "On the Jews and Their Lies" in which he says that the Jews are a "base whoring people, that is, no people of God, and their boast of lineage, circumcision, and law must be accounted as filth. They are full of the devil's feces...which they wallow in like swine." He wrote that their synagogue was a "defiled bride, yes, and incorrigible whore and evil slut..." He then argues in his writings that their synagogues and schools be set on fire, their prayer books destroyed and money confiscated.

In his effort to eliminate these Oneness people, he continued in his writing to say, "They should be shown no mercy or kindness, afforded no legal protection, and these poisonous envenomed worms should be drafted into forced labor or expelled for all times."

Martin Luther also advocated the murder of the children of Abraham by saying, "We are at fault in not slaying them."

This reformer was a German citizen and lived four hundred years before the second World War. Was an anti-Semitic spirit against the Jews already flowing through the veins of German society when the war began? Was Martin Luther the reformer actually the forerunner of Adolf Hitler? Yes, he was!

If Martin Luther had been a true **Son of God** would he have demanded the death of the men, women, and children that believed in the monotheistic God of Abraham? The truth of the matter is that he was NOT a **Son of God.** He was a **Son of Man** leading *man-made* religious Christianity into deeper darkness. Did Martin Luther not read in his Bible that God is a God of love and long suffering? Jesus could have called ten thousand angels to destroy the Jews and the Roman soldiers, but chose to have mercy on them all.

The job to rid the world of Michael Servetus, the human thorn that penetrated the side of *man-made* religious Christianity, would fall to the hands of John Calvin. This individual who lived in the days of Michael Servetus was regarded as one of the chief leaders of the Protestant Reformation.

Even though John Calvin campaigned against the obvious corruption and many false teachings of the Catholic Church, he, like Martin Luther, continued to support Tertullian's belief that there were three separate identities in the Godhead.

John Calvin, the founding father of the Presbyterian Church, detested the Oneness convictions of Servetus, and eventually had him burned to death in Geneva, Switzerland.

John Calvin, did you not read your Bible? Burning people to death is not part of the Christian faith, unless of course you are part of *man-made* religious Christianity that was and is being led by the **Sons of Man**.

This reformer of the sixteenth century is responsible for the "Once saved always saved" doctrine. Today in *man-made* religious Christianity you hear, "accept the Lord Jesus as your personal Saviour and you will be saved."

It is not about us accepting Him, it is about Him accepting us!

> "For many are called but few
> are chosen."

Matthew 22:14

If I knew the wealthiest man on this planet and wanted to be his son, it would be very easy for me to accept him as my father. However, it would do me no good in the end if he did not accept me as his son. Without him accepting me I could never be his heir.

For God to accept one as His son, that person must become a **Son of God** through the New Birth which will in turn make them an heir and joint-heir with Christ.

The rest of the story about Michael Servetus, the Oneness martyr, is a tale of horror. Death at the stake over a slow fire was the most agonizing of all modes of execution. Green wood was intentionally used to slow the fire and extend the agony of the consumed.

As the crowd gathered, on October 27, 1553, Michael Servetus was dragged from the darkness of his sixteenth century dungeon. His imprisonment had left him in a filthy and impoverished condition. Feeling the sharp, cruel claws of reality clamping down upon him and being irretrievably broken by Pope Julius III and John Calvin, he lowered his head as his accusers read these words:

"We condemn thee, Michael Servetus, to be conveyed in bonds to your place of execution, there to be burned alive, and with thee the manuscript of thy book and the printed volume, until thy body is consumed to ashes. Thus thou shalt end thy days, as a warning to all others who might wish to repeat thine offence."

Servetus felt the coarsely hewed timber scrape across his back as he was pressed firmly against the wooden stake. The heavy chain attached to the stake was then pulled tightly four or five times around Servetus's emaciated body. It seemed with each constrictive pass death drew even closer. Between the links of chain and the alive but wasted body of Michael Servetus, were placed his book and his manuscript pertaining to his Oneness convictions. Finally, in a harsh spirit of scorn, a crown of leaves was placed upon his brow. The leaves had been soaked in sulfur. The wood was kindled and the murder began. When the flames of torment burst forth from the green wood, Michael Servetus, the man who would not recant, knowing that there was only One person in the Godhead, uttered so dreadful a cry that many of his onlookers hid their eyes from the pitiful sight.

This man's struggle with death lasted for half an hour. Once the shrill screams of agony subsided, above the glowing embers could be seen the black, sickening, charred mass, which had lost all human resemblance. Michael Servetus was forty-two years old at the time of his death.

One day while living in the country of Switzerland, I was asked to preach in Geneva. I felt so honored to preach this One God Apostolic message on the ground that was partially formulated by the ashes of Michael Servetus.

Now let's pick up where Michael Servetus left off. If the truth was known, we who today support the Oneness of God would likewise have been burned to death if we were living in the days of Pope Julius III.

For the next while, we will be taking a hard look at this *man-made* church that harbored the trinity doctrine as early as the second century.

Monotheism has meant Oneness from the beginning of time. Trinitarianism has meant three and teaches that there are three separate identities within the Godhead. Is there one God or are there three Gods? Is there one nature or are there three natures in one? Will we see one identity in heaven, or will we see three separate identities? What is the true nature and identity of Almighty God? Do we support monotheism, or do we support polytheism as they did in the Roman Empire?

> "Remember the former things
> of old: for I am God, and there is
> none else; I am God, and there is
> none like me."

Isaiah 46:9

The empire that started in Rome could be divided up into four different titles over a long period of time. To be exact, from 753 B.C. until August 6, 1806. A.D. The empire started in a small town called Rome in 753 B.C. known as the Roman Kingdom. It then took on the name of the

Roman Republic, the Roman Empire, and finally the Holy Roman Empire, which was dissolved by Napoleon Bonaparte in 1806.

Prior to the birth of the Messiah, only the Jews believed in the monotheistic nature of the God of Abraham. It was the Imperial cult that ruled the land. Polytheism had been the mentality of the empire for centuries. The emperors were themselves often deified.

While at the Trappist monastery at Oka, Quebec, and at he Seminary of Theology in New Brunswick, a lot of my time was spent trying to understand the trinity. It proved to be very, very confusing to myself, to other seminarians, and to the priests that taught us the doctrine as well.

At the end of the day, it always fell on the same scapegoat, "It is a mystery that is beyond our ability to comprehend." Now that I have the Holy Ghost and have been baptized in Jesus' Name, I understand that it is a mystery, but a mystery only to those who have not received the revelation from God Himself. There is a world of difference between the **Sons of God** and the **Sons of Man**. Be not deceived in this midnight hour. God does not toy in riddles with mortal man that He gave His life for at Calvary!

"All things are delivered unto me of my Father, and no man knoweth the Son, but the Father; neither knoweth any man the Father, save the Son, and He [those who through the New Birth became the **Sons of God**] to whomsoever the Son will reveal him."

Matthew 11:27

The Godhead is not complicated, but actually quite simple. It is, however, understood only through Divine revelation.

Salvation does not start with God, a church, Sunday School, a Bible study, an invitation to God's house, or with a preacher. Salvation starts with a hungry heart and God in His great love is drawn to hunger. Salvation is God's response to a hungry heart!

It is time that the Roman Catholic Church and all those associated with *man-made* religious Christianity look within and sincerely seek a genuine hunger for the things of God. No one can go to heaven without the New Birth experience. It really doesn't matter what people think or say. It is not your education that is going to get you to heaven, even though we respect those who are educated. To go to heaven, one must wholeheartedly embrace the Unadulterated Word of God.

Who is being led by the **Sons of God** and who is being led by the **Sons of Man**? We need to have a very clear understanding now—not when we stand before our eternal and righteous Judge.

> "Behold, what manner of love the Father hath bestowed upon us, that we should be called the **Sons of God**: therefore, the world knoweth us not, because it knew him not."

> I John 3:1

Although the Roman Empire was pagan in the days of the Messiah, it is important to acknowledge that throughout history, the Lord fervently warned and continued to warn His people about falling into the graven sin of idolatry and insisted that He would not share His glory with another identity. This is not a witch-hunt, but any teaching in the church's two thousand years of history that offers anything outside of His monotheistic nature offers their followers only blasphemous theology.

My confusion deepened when I realized at the seminary that my church—the Roman Catholic Church with her well-educated theologians—was actually teaching contrary to our own doctrine concerning the Godhead. The trinity doctrine absolutely and without question defies understanding! As time goes on, you will understand my confusion as I struggled to understand why the Vatican insists that there are three separate identities in the Godhead when our own Catholic Encyclopedia and our greatest theologians taught against it. God is not the author of confusion. Man is the author of confusion. As a Catholic seminarian, I was searching and trying to comprehend but had no one to show me the way.

According to the *New Catholic Encyclopedia*, we witness an ongoing contradiction in the church's doctrine.

    1. The formation "One God in three persons" was NOT solidly established, certainly not fully assimilated into Christian life and its profession of faith, prior to the end of the fourth century.

    2. The Old Testament clearly DOES NOT envisage God's

Spirit as a person—God's Spirit is simply God's power.

3. The majority of New Testament texts reveal God's Spirit as something, NOT someone. This is especially seen in the parallelism between the Spirit and the power of God.

New Catholic Encyclopedia,
1965, "Spirit of God"

In one of my classes on Roman Catholic Theology, I was taught trinitarian-monotheism. My question to the professor was sincerely firm. How can we believe in trinitarian-monotheism when the trinity speaks of three while monotheism speaks of one?

The trinity doctrine has confused sincere hearts seeking the God of Abraham from the third century and beyond, as noted in the following statement:

"There are few teachers of trinitarian theology in the Catholic seminaries who have not been badgered at one time or another by the question, but how does one teach the trinity? And if the question is symptomatic of confusion on the part of the students, perhaps it is no less symptomatic of similar confusion on the part of their professors."

New Catholic Encyclopedia,
1965, "Trinity"

At the end of these classes it was always an open forum for anyone's input. It seemed that the professors were always hoping for a ray of insight into the matter themselves, from the students.

As the years went by at the seminary, my confusion concerning the Godhead only deepened. Were my professors confused by the trinity doctrine as well? Yes, they were! They were also looking for a logical explanation.

The teaching on the subject of the Godhead always proved to be contradictory. Monotheism has meant Oneness since the beginning of time. The truth of the matter is quite simple. There have *never* been three separate identities in the Godhead; there *are not* three separate identities in the Godhead; and there *will never be* three separate identities in the Godhead. So where did this previously unheard of doctrine come from? Hello, it was from the **Sons of Man**!

I have a question for you as we get back to the New Birth that Jesus talked about to Nicademous. Is it the **Sons of God** who are leading the Pure Apostolic Church, telling the **Sons of Man** that are leading *man-made* religious Christianity that there are not three separate identities in the Godhead, or is it the **Sons of Man** telling the **Sons of God** that there are not three separate identities in the Godhead?

When I was at the seminary of Philosophy, an announcement was made at the dinner table that Rev. John L. McKenzie had just received the much coveted Cardinal Spellman Award.

John L. McKenzie was a Jesuit Biblical scholar in the Roman Catholic Church. He taught for many years at DePaul University in Chicago and was awarded the Cardinal Spellman Award in 1967. He was the first president of the Society of Biblical Literature and a past president of the Catholic Biblical Society.

It does not matter who you are or what name is tacked over your church door. When one turns to the Bible, things are always seen differently!

This Roman Catholic scholar could speak eleven languages fluently and was recognized in Rome as one of the most outstanding professors of higher learning in the history of the church.

The man's legacy, however, is well-remembered as the outspoken leader that accused the Roman Catholic Church of tampering in the early years of the church with the internal intent of Jesus' words in order to accommodate violence towards non-Catholics.

I felt a genuine hunger from within to understand the truth concerning the nature of the God of Abraham. The question that I repeatedly asked was directed at my professors and was actually quite simple in nature: Are we to believe as students of Roman Catholic theology that the creeds of the church and the twenty-one ecumenical councils over the past two thousand years are more Orthodox than the Holy Bible? The answer was always the same. "I guess." To me, guessing at such an important matter was not an educated answer. I am sure that I was not the most popular student among the professors or among the other students as far as that goes. But I could not cope with contradiction. I could not cope with it then, nor can I cope with it now. To me it is, or it is not!

The following statement on the topic of the trinity is by Rev. John L. McKenzie, from his *Dictionary of the Bible*.

> "The trinity of God is defined by the Catholic Church as the belief that in God are three persons who subsist in one nature. The belief as so defined was reached only in the fourth and fifth centuries A.D., and hence is NOT explicitly and formally a Biblical belief. The trinity of persons within the unity of nature is defined in the terms "person and nature," which are Greek philosophical terms; actually the terms do not appear in the Bible. The trinitarian definitions arose as a result of long controversies in which these terms and other such as "essence" and "substance" were erroneously [wrongly] applied to God by some theologians of that day..."

> *Dictionary of the Bible*,
> page 899

Jesus the Messiah insisted that there was but One God. He supported His own monotheistic nature because He was the only Father, the only God, and the only Lord. As is found in the book of Mark, the Lord quoted the writings of Moses found in Deuteronomy 6:4.

> "And Jesus answered him, The first of all the commandments is Hear, O Israel: The Lord our God is ONE Lord."

Mark 12:29

It appears that God was putting a special emphasis on this particular commandment.

All Christendom has been torn by a dispute regarding the trinity since it was conceived in the mind of Tertullian in the second century. In the fourth century, Emperor Theodious I outlawed the terminology that Jesus used, "The Lord our God is one Lord," as being contrary to the trinity doctrine. He made his decree civil law at the second ecumenical council in 381 A.D. at Constantinople.

Although my outspokenness was not appreciated by some, I am sure, I needed an answer to my questions. Do we believe in the doctrine of the trinity, or not? I did not get a proper or educated answer until God revealed Himself to me at an Apostolic Church. The trinity

66

doctrine was not the work of the **Sons of God** but the writings of the **Sons of Man** professing true Christianity.

It is recorded in history that Tertullian coined the word "trinity." He may have introduced the word to Christianity, but it had been in existence long before his theory of the nature of the God of Abraham.

Most religions on earth are polytheistic in nature. Polytheism is not new to the world and was practiced in India long before the trinity doctrine was slowly absorbed into what we know today as *man-made* religious Christianity. Hinduism is one of the oldest religions on earth where their TRINITY doctrine has been perpetually taught for many, many centuries, before the birth of the Messiah.

The Hindu trinity is very similar to the trinity doctrine that is taught outside of the Apostolic Church.

In Hindu reckoning, their trinity doctrine is made up of Brahma, Vishnu, and Shiva. They are respectively the creator, preserver, and destroyer of the universe. They are aligned as the transcendent godhead.

Each god in the Hindu trinity has his consort. For Brahma, she is the goddess of knowledge; for Vishnu, the goddess of love, beauty, and delight; and for Shiva, the goddess of power, destruction, and transformation. These three identities are openly venerated within the faith of Hinduism.

I have often wondered why sinners celebrate the birth and resurrection of Christ. Only Buddhists celebrate the birth of Buddha, and only Hindus celebrate the feasts of their gods within Hinduism. I guess it is simply part of *man-made* religious Christianity. The **Sons of God** should be the only ones celebrating Christmas!

The Mormons teach and practice polytheism. On the issue of the trinity, the Godhead is explained by their founder Joseph Smith as follows:

> "I have always declared God to be a distinct personage, Jesus Christ a separate and distinct personage from God the Father, and the Holy Ghost was a distinct personage and a Spirit: and these three constitute three distinct personages and three Gods."

Teaching of Joseph Smith, p. 370

Although I do not believe that there are three Gods, one must give Joseph Smith credit in the matter. He did believe in the trinity, but did not deny polytheism, as do others.

In contrast to the teaching of Joseph Smith, the Jehovah Witnesses teach monotheism as do those in Judaism and in the Pure Apostolic Church. On the issue of the trinity doctrine of Tertullian, the Jehovah Witnesses lead by Rev. Charles Taze Russell declared that:

> "Never was there a more deceptive doctrine advanced than that of the trinity. It could have originated only in one mind, and that the mind of Satan the Devil."

Reconciliation, 1928, p. 101

Monotheism means Oneness in its entirety. We must understand the true nature of our Lord and Saviour Jesus Christ. If anyone believes that there are three separate identities in the Godhead, they are without doubt members of the *man-made* Christian church that supports polytheism—not monotheism—that God emphatically warned Israel about!

The teaching of the Unity of God or the Oneness of God was greatly emphasized by

Eastern theologians through the detailed writings of Irenaeus, who lived in the second century. *Against Heresies* is a five volume work written by Irenaeus. A couple of excerpts from his work are:

> "It is proper, then, that I should begin with the first and most important head, that is God the creator, who made the heavens and the earth and all things that are therein, and to demonstrate that there is nothing either above Him or after Him, nor that influenced by anyone [no other person] but of His own free will. He created all things, since He is the Only God, the only Lord, the only Creator, the only Father, alone containing all things and Himself commanding all things into existence."

> Book II Ch. I, VI

> "The Holy Spirit and the Christ, being the hands of God the Father, reaching from the infinite into the finite."

> Book III, Ch. IX, III

This theologian of the second century understood as did others the Sovereignty of Almighty God.

> "Thus sayeth the Lord, thy redeemer, and he that formed thee from the womb, I am the Lord that maketh all things: that stretcheth forth the heavens alone; that spreadeth abroad the earth by myself."

> Isaiah 44:24

I was a Roman Catholic and it amazes me that the Protestant Churches that emerged from the reformation are so adamantly against Catholicism and at the same time support her doctrine of the trinity.

It is time that all people sincerely seeking truth concerning the true nature of the God of Abraham get back to the simplicity of the New Birth. No human being at any point in history will ever distort what God Himself implemented.

When Isaiah was writing about God stretching forth the heavens alone; that spreadeth abroad the earth by Himself, was he referring to Jesus Christ? Absolutely!

"He was in the world, and the world was made by HIM, and the world knew Him not."

John 1:10

There has been a lot of talk about the love of our Lord toward us. Is it possible to actually fathom the agape love of the One, True, and Living God? In our search to do so, we must go deeper.

If we really believe that Jesus Christ the prophesied Messiah was indeed God incarnate, we must also be prepared to believe that He walked on the water He alone created. He bled on a cross that was fashioned from a tree He spoke into existence; and by the swipe of His hand He created a hill the Jews referred to as Golgotha knowing that one day in mortal time for you and I He would walk up it as the Lamb of God.

Chapter Three: Creeds and Councils

We have been talking about the two churches representing Christianity: The Pure Apostolic Church that understands the Sovereignty of God and the *man-made* Christian church that is still trying to understand the doctrine of the trinity. It is time for the **Sons of Man** to GET OVER IT and sincerely get back to the New Birth and become a **Son of God!** The revelation of who Jesus really is comes from the Divine. It does not come from man's creeds and his carnal councils. The Lord did not have any intention to divide nor did He during the history of His Church cause division within. Men divided his blood-washed church. Almost from the birth of the church Satan saw to it that the house of believers was divided as were the twelve tribes of Israel divided in the days of King Rehoboam.

"But Peter and John answered
and said unto them, Whether it be
right in the sight of God to hearken

> unto you more than unto God, judge ye."

Acts 4:19

Prior to the fourth century, paganism was the faith that was practiced in the Roman Empire that promoted the Imperial Cult. The Pure Apostolic Church was illegal in the empire and was underground. Emperors like Titus and Nero were feeding Apostolics to the lions at the Coliseum and at the Circus of Nero for their entertainment.

I go to the country of China often and understand what it means to teach this amazing truth in their underground churches. What we believe is illegal in China. It was likewise illegal in the Roman Empire in the days of the Apostles.

Constantine the Great was the first Christian Emperor in the Roman Empire. He was the best thing that could have happened to the Saints of God seeing that he made their faith legal in the Empire. For almost three hundred years the Apostolic people struggling underground with their monotheistic convictions watching as those they loved were fed to hungry lions.

On the other hand, Constantine was the worst thing that could have happened to the Apostolic Church because it was now to be *Ecclesia vivit lege romana*—The church lives under Roman law. No changes would be made in the church without the permission of the Roman Emperor. The first seven ecumenical councils of the church were not called by the bishops of Rome or Constantinople, but by the very powerful emperors residing in Constantinople. The church would be controlled by these emperors for the next almost five hundred years.

The first seven ecumenical councils called by the heads of state are as follows:

1. First Council of Nicaea—called by Emperor Constantine I in 325 A.D.

2. First Council of Constantinople—called by Emperor Theodosius I in 381 A.D.

3. Council of Ephesus—called by Emperor Theodosius II in 431 A.D.

4. Council of Chalcedon—called by Emperor Marcion in 451 A.D.

5. Second Council of Constantinople—called by Emperor Justinian in 553 A.D.

6. Third Council of Constantinople—called by Emperor Constantine IV in 680 A.D.

7. Second Council of Nicaea—called by Empress Irene of Athens in 787 A.D.

Guess what the first ecumenical council at Nicaea Turkey called by Emperor Constantine I was all about. It was about the Sovereignty of Christ and the much debated trinity doctrine that was trying desperately to make its way into the Pure Apostolic Church. The empire was divided over the issues and seeing that it was the emperor's job to maintain tranquility among his subjects, he called the council to settle the issues. Bishop Nicholas from the east was present at this council. History reveals that Bishop Nicholas, the trinitarian bishop, became violent at the council and actually struck Arias (the theologian for whom the 3rd and 4th century theology promoting "Arianism"—the Oneness of God—was named) as he spoke in defense of the Oneness of God. Bishop Nicholas was later seen as a holy man by the *man-made* church and who later became known to the world as Santa Claus.

The emperors now head of the church were often seen in the empire as deities themselves. The true church with its freedom would prove to be short lived. Because of the decision of the first ecumenical council at Nicaea on the Godhead, the Apostolic Church would once again be forced underground not being willing to compromise the Oneness of God.

The birth of the *man-made* Christian church that could not then or today take the place of His blood-washed church, was quickly becoming insensitive to the Holy Word of God. The Roman Empire was quickly becoming a theocracy at the expense of the gospel.

The subjects of the empire then believed that God was speaking to the emperors on their behalf. These emperors were referred to as being the "Greatest Bridge Builders." That is, they were to be the mediators between humanity and Divinity.

We are not talking here about the humble anointed spirit of Christ and His Apostles any more that taught you to love your neighbor. We are talking about the most powerful man governing the most powerful empire on earth. These men were dictators who wholeheartedly embraced totalitarianism. A totalitarian such as was Adolf Hitler crushes all autonomous institutions in its drive or quest to seize the human soul.

The man that called the first of the twenty-one ecumenical councils may have been the emperor, but was very unseasoned in Christian theology. He was considered by the church as a catechumen—an individual that studies questions and answers of the faith. This newly converted emperor was not baptized until he was baptized on his death bed. This leads me to believe that he had never rally experienced the New Birth and would be instrumental in the formation of the *man-made* church that was tailored to meet the carnal needs of the **Sons of Man**.

Within a year of the Council of Nicaea, Constantine the Great had his oldest son Crispus executed because of a rumor that the boy had an affair with his second wife Fausta. Constantine's mother informed Constantine after the fact that it was his second wife's decision to start the rumor so that her son could succeed Constantine on the Imperial throne. This individual that promoted the trinity doctrine then had his second wife Fausta executed as the apparent source of the rumor. This emperor had obviously not experienced the New Birth in his lifetime that would have made him a **Son of God**.

Remember, at this point in the Roman Empire as it was previously in the Roman Kingdom and the Roman Republic, the dominating mentality was that the emperors were themselves seen as gods and were worshipped accordingly. If any angel or human being is a **Son of God**, it is because they were born of the Spirit of God. God's message to the emperors: "Ye Must Be Born Again."

Eusebuis Pamphili of Caesarea became the bishop of Caesarea Palaestina in 314 A.D. and is often referred to in history as the Father of Church History. He enjoyed a lavish lifestyle and the friendship of Emperor Constantine I. He was also prominent in the transaction during the First Nicene Council in 325 A.D. Eusebius clearly showed how the emperor's presence was deified as he entered the council with pomp and power when he said:

"Constantine himself proceeded through the midst of the assembly, like some heavenly messenger from God, clothed in raiment which glittered as if it were rays of light, reflecting the glowing radiance of a purple robe, and adorned with brilliant splendor of gold and precious stones."

It is very easy to see how the leaders of the Roman Empire held a very tight reign on the church for such a long period of time. Though Emperor Constantine's conversion gave a glimmer of hope to the Apostolic Church, it would quickly prove to be a bitter-sweet experience for them.

Emperor Constantine with his pagan mentality approved of the trinity doctrine, however, because of the challenges from the **Sons of God** who were eventually forced to go back underground, the trinity doctrine would not be ratified for fifty-six years down the road at the first council in Constantinople in the year 381 A.D.

Emperor Theodosus I called the second ecumenical council at Constantinople to settle the much debated doctrine of the trinity. The doctrine of the trinity was not only ratified by this council but Theodosus I made the doctrine civil law in the empire. The emperor's decree in 381 A.D.

"The doctrine of the trinity is to be the official state belief and that all subjects shall adhere to it."

Emperor Theodosus I was not only head of the Roman Empire, but the head of the Christian Church as well. There was no separation of church and state and would not be for another fifteen hundred years, not even in the Holy Roman Empire, up until well into the eighteenth and nineteenth centuries when the pontiffs of Rome and Avignon ruled. The doctrine of the trinity became civil law in the empire and perpetrators who chose to challenge the decree were immediately seen as heretics and executed. There was a zero tolerance in the emperor's kingdom.

The blood-washed church with its Pentecostal experience was now once again forced underground. This time it would not be for three hundred years but for many, many centuries to come.

While the Pure Apostolic Church with its Acts 2:38 message led by the **Sons of God** went into hiding, the new *man*-made Christian Church that was being led by the **Sons of Man** flourished under the emperor's leadership.

In 2016, for this *man-made* church to obtain salvation, they must get back to the Born Again experience. This experience will lead them as it has led others to the knowledge of who the Messiah really was. It is still "Ye Must Be Born Again!"

Although there were heresies practically from the beginning, the birth of this new *man-made* church that still exists in our day was actually put in motion by Emperor Theodosus I. The trinity doctrine for Apostolics was the dividing line! Although persecuted, the church was protected by the nail-scarred hands of the God of Abraham.

Before the seventh century, there were seven creeds written within this *man-made* church, each one with its own additions and omissions. Now the real question requires an educated answer. Were the authors of these creeds the **Sons of God** that had experienced the New Birth that was set in motion in the first century, or were they the **Sons of Man** who had not experienced Christ's New Birth but were leaning on the arm of flesh?

The seven creeds prior to the seventh century are as follows:

1. The Roman or Old Roman Creed
2. The Apostles Creed
3. The Nicene Creed
4. The Creed of Constantinople
5. The Creed of Jerusalem
6. The Chalcedonian Creed
7. The Atheniasian Creed

For your convenience and knowledge, I shall write the first and last of these creeds. The Roman Creed that pre-dates the rule of Emperor Constantine I mentions nothing about a trinity doctrine, while the Atheniasian Creed under the watchful eye of the emperor talks almost exclusively about this trinity doctrine. To the degree that one cannot be saved without the belief.

To believe in the monotheistic God of Abraham when the Atheniasian Creed was written was seen as heresy in the empire. It was against the inseparable church and state.

First the Roman or Old Roman Creed in its simplicity, explaining God's activity. Nothing is mentioned about a Catholic Church or a trinity:

Roman Creed—2nd Century A.D.

"I believe in God the Father Almighty; and in Christ Jesus His only Son, our Lord, who was born of the Holy Spirit and the virgin Mary, who under Pontius Pilate was crucified and buried, On the third day rose again from the dead, ascended to heaven, sits at the right hand of the Father, whence He will come to judge the living and the dead, and in the Holy Spirit, the holy church, the remission of sins, the resurrection of the flesh (the life everlasting)."

Now that the trinity doctrine was made civil law, it appears that the church fathers were eager to accommodate the wishes of the emperors. For them to stay alive, a choice was imminent. Go underground with the unpopular **Sons of God** or hold your peace among the **Sons of Man**.

Now you will witness the complicated Atheniasian Creed that was written by the **Sons of Man** under the watchful eye of the man that led the most powerful empire on earth:

Atheniasian Creed—6th Century A.D.

"Whosoever will be saved, before all things it is necessary that he hold the catholic faith. Which faith except every one do keep whole and undefiled, without doubt he shall perish everlastingly.

"And the catholic faith is this, that we worship one God in Trinity, and Trinity in Unity; Neither confounding the Persons, nor dividing the Substance. For there is one Person of the Father, another of the Son, and another of the Holy Ghost. But the Godhead of the Father, of the Son, and of the Holy Ghost is all one: the glory equal, the majesty coeternal. Such as the Father is, such is the Son, and such is the Holy Ghost. The Father uncreated, the Son uncreated, and the Holy Ghost uncreated. The Father incomprehensible, the Son incomprehensible, and the Holy Ghost incomprehensible. The Father eternal, the Son eternal, and the Holy Ghost eternal. And yet they are not three Eternals, but one Eternal. As there are not three Uncreated nor three Incomprehensibles, but one Uncreated and one Incomprehensible. So likewise the Father is almighty, the Son almighty, and the Holy Ghost almighty. And yet they are not three Almighties, but one Almighty. So the Father is God, the Son is God, and the Holy Ghost is God. And yet they are not three Gods, but one God. So likewise the Father is Lord, the Son Lord, and the Holy Ghost Lord. And yet not three Lords, but one Lord. For like as we are compelled by the Christian verity to acknowledge every Person by Himself to be God and Lord, So are we forbidden by the catholic religion to say, There be three Gods, or three Lords.

"The Father is made of none: neither created nor begotten. The Son is of the Father alone; not made, nor created, but begotten. The Holy Ghost is of the Father and of the Son: neither made, nor created, nor begotten, but proceeding. So there is one Father, not three Fathers; one Son, not three Sons; one Holy Ghost, not three Holy Ghosts. And in this Trinity none is before or after another; none is greater or less than another; But the whole three Persons are coeternal together, and coequal: so that in all things, as is aforesaid, the Unity in Trinity and the Trinity in Unity is to be worshiped. He, therefore, that will be saved must thus think of the Trinity.

"Furthermore, it is necessary to everlasting salvation that he also believe faithfully the incarnation of our Lord Jesus Christ. For the right faith is, that we believe and confess that our Lord Jesus Christ, the Son of God, is God and Man; God of the Substance of the Father, begotten before the worlds; and Man of the substance of His mother, born in the world; [John L. McKenzie the Roman Catholic Jesuit priest was talking about these words 'essence' and 'persons' when he said that they were wrongly used in the creed and that the trinity doctrine was NOT explicitly a Biblical belief.] Perfect God and perfect Man, of a reasonable soul and human flesh subsisting. Equal to the Father as touching His Godhead, and inferior to the Father as touching His manhood; Who, although He be God and Man, yet He is not two, but one Christ: One, not by conversion of the Godhead into flesh, but by taking the manhood into God; One altogether; not by confusion of Substance, but by unity of Person. For as the reasonable soul and flesh is one man, so God and Man is one Christ; Who suffered for our salvation; descended into hell, rose again the third day from the dead; He ascended into heaven; He sitteth on the right hand of the Father, God Almighty; from whence He shall come to judge the quick and the dead. At whose coming all men shall rise again with their bodies, and shall give an account of their own works. And they that have done good shall go into life everlasting; and they that have done evil, into everlasting fire.

"This is the catholic faith; which except a man believe faithfully and firmly, he cannot be saved."

When I was studying the Atheniasian Creed not as an Apostolic individual with the Holy Ghost, but as a Roman Catholic person studying Catholic Theology, I found myself sitting back in my chair. I was thinking at that time someone spent a lot of time trying to prove to others that the trinity doctrine was right when they did not believe or understand the theory themselves.

When Pope Boniface VII came to power in Rome, he, in a effort to maintain unity within the Catholic Church and assert dominance throughout the world, issued a papal bull (papal document) in 1302 A.D. called "Unam Sanctam." This document stated that: "To obtain salvation every human being must be subject to the pope."

As I write today, my message to Pope Boniface and to the current pontiff is this: Just because the Roman Catholic Church said it, does not make it so. *Man-made* religious Christianity run by and followed by the **Sons of Man** is fated to cease in the end-time. It is not time for every human being to be subject to the Pope. It is time that every human being get back to the New Birth experience that is clearly outlined in the book of the Acts of the Apostles. It is still repentance, it is still baptism in Jesus' Name and it is still the baptism of the Holy Ghost with the evidence of speaking in other tongues. To be saved, we must get back to the Bible that was written by the **Sons of God**.

What happened between the second century and the sixth and seventh centuries? The keys to the kingdom of God were taken from the hands of Peter and placed in the hands of the emperors and later in the hands of the pontiffs of Rome and Avignon!

Back to the trinity doctrine. Doxology is from the Greek word meaning "glory" and is an ascription of praise to the three persons or three identities in the trinity. A common medieval tradition founded on a spurious letter of St. Jerome (in the Benedictine edition, Paris, v.415) says that Bishop Damasus I introduced the *Gloria Patri* in the late fourth century.

That is:

- ❖ Glory be to the Father
- ❖ Glory be to the Son
- ❖ Glory be to the Holy Spirit

The man who coined the word trinity in what would become a *man-made* church dogma was none other than Quintus Septimus Florens Tertullianus. This theologian is better known in history as Tertullian that lived in the third century.

Tertullian not only taught the people that there were three separate identities in the Godhead, but also taught traducianism which claimed that the soul of man did not come from God but from his parents.

Tertullian taught against such renowned Greek philosophical doctors as Socrates and Plato. He called Aristotle a patriarchal forefather of heretics. Tertullian was eventually ex-communicated from the church.

"Ye are my witnesses, saith the Lord, and my servant whom I have chosen: that ye may know and believe me, and understand that I am he: before me there was no God formed, neither shall there be after me. I, even I, am the Lord; and beside me there is no saviour."

Isaiah 43:10-11

The trinity doctrine was birthed in the Roman Empire within the union of Apostolic compromise and political dominance. I am not writing to satisfy a vindictive spirit, but I understand that in my sincerity I was absolutely walking down the wrong road.

We must not be wise in our own eyes. It can not be about what "I think that I understand." To become a **Son of God**, one must not be void of the sincerity and driving hunger that is required to do so. The elements of sincerity and hunger are not optional as we make our way to the altar of repentance.

We must likewise be advised that it is not God nor is it the **Son of God** who so often experiences confusion and blurred vision concerning His identity. It is the **Sons of Man** professing Christianity as I was that experience confusion in comprehending the Lord's identity as well as His sovereignty.

Can God hide absolute truth from those individuals that may be less than sincere? Could He actually hide His identity? It appears to me that He has the ability to do so.

> "In that hour Jesus rejoiced in spirit, and said, I thank thee, O Father, Lord of heaven and earth that thou has hid these things from the wise and prudent and hast revealed them unto babes: even so, Father, for so it seemed good in thy sight."

> Luke10:21

The scripture "Hear, O Israel: The Lord our God is one Lord: And thou shalt love the Lord thy God with all thine heart, and with all thy soul, and with all thy might" that is found in Deuteronomy 6:4-5 absolutely and blatantly defies the doctrine of the trinity. To believe that there are three separate identities in the Godhead sharing God's glory is blasphemy.

Chapter Four: Back to His Church

While studying for the priesthood, I can honestly say that I was very sincere in what I was trying to do and what I was selflessly trying to be. Whatever the cost, we must never condemn people of other faiths that do not know Him in the power of the Holy Ghost. At that time in my life I did not know any Apostolic people. I had no connection with the Apostolic Church, therefore I had no one to show me the way to salvation. However, I did not accidentally stumble across the truth. I believe that I was led out of a very dark place by the illuminating Spirit of God to know and to understand the truth.

Salvation does not start with God but He is drawn to hunger. Salvation is God's response to a hungry heart that He alone understands.

I absolutely and positively believe in the power that lies in the spontaneous and intercessory prayers of God's people, the **Sons of God**.

One evening while thumbing my rosary and venerating the Virgin Mary, I felt that someone somewhere was praying for me. Yet being caught up in *man-made* religion, I could not understand why. I supported ritualism. I loved my traditions and formal worship. I did not know the power of the Holy Ghost, had never felt His presence, and believed myself to be in the will of God. In my daily devotion, I faithfully prayed to the medieval saints that I now understand could neither hear nor answer my prayers. Let me pause for a moment to address the title ("The Queen of Heaven") given to the mother of Jesus by my former church.

It is imperative that we caution hungry hearts searching for truth about the real danger of blasphemous theology.

In the book of Jeremiah, God warns Judah of the danger of yielding to gods within the framework of cultism. At that time in history, He was not referring to the mother of the prophesied Christ. He was referring to the gods in the land which were silent to the cries of the people.

> "The children gather wood, and the fathers kindle the fire, and the women kneed their dough, to make cakes to the "Queen of Heaven," and to pour out drink

offerings unto other gods, that they
may provoke me to anger."

Jeremiah 7:18

The "Queen of Heaven" was a title given to a number of ancient goddesses in the ancient world of cultism and even in the realms of demonology. In modern history, the title is still being used across the globe.

Lucius Apuleius (124-170 A.D.) was a Latin pose writer who was well traveled in his day. He studied philosophy in Athens, Greece. His most famous work was the novel, "The Golden Ass." In this novel, Book II, Chapter 47, his character prayed to the Queen of Heaven. A picture of Lucius being transformed back into human form in a 1345 A.D. illustration can be seen in the Apostolic library at the Vatican in Rome.

> "Lucius wakes up in a panic during the first watch of the night. Considering fate to be done tormenting him, he takes the opportunity to purify himself by seven consecutive immersions in the sea. He then offers a prayer to the "Queen of Heaven" for his return to human form, citing all the

various names of the goddesses
known by the people everywhere.
The queen of Heaven appears in a
vision to him and explains to him
how he can be returned to human
form by eating the crown of roses
that will be held by one of the
priests during a religious
procession the following day.
Lucius follows her instructions and
is returned to human form and, at
length, initiated into her
priesthood."

On January 24, 1998, Pope John Paul II
personally crowned a statue in the country of Cuba
and declared Mary the mother of Jesus as being
the "Queen of Cuba." Thousands of Roman
Catholic pilgrims lined up to kiss the feet of the
statue.

In Roman Catholic Mariology, the mother of
Jesus is referred to as being the mother of God and
thus is essential to the final, spiritual perfection of
every creature. According to this church dogma,
Mary's involvement in salvation makes her co-
redemptrix along with her son Jesus Christ. It is
firmly believed in Rome that Mary the "Queen of
Heaven" along with her son atones for our sins.

The title "Mother of God" was given to Mary during the third ecumenical council at Ephesis in 431 A.D., which was called by Emperor Theodosius II. This Roman Emperor was the grandson of Emperor Theodosius I, who made the trinity doctrine civil law in 381 A.D. at the second ecumenical council at Constantinople.

In 1854, Pope Pius IX declared that Mary, the mother of Jesus, never had original sin at her birth, nor did she acquire elements of original sin during the course of her lifetime.

In 1950, Pope Pius XII, through Ex-Cathedra (from the throne) declared through his believed infallible office that Mary never went by the way of the grave but was assumed up into heaven as was Enoch and the prophet Elijah.

When I was studying for the priesthood, I unwaveringly prayed to the "Queen of Heaven." Did I anger God as they did in the days of Jeremiah who lived over 2700 years ago?

Mary never was, never wanted to be, and will never be a mexiatrix between humanity and Divinity. She knew in hear heart what the Jewish prophet Isaiah recorded in words: God alone is Saviour.

> "I, even I, am the Lord; and beside me there is no saviour."

> Isaiah 43:11

Who will stand accountable for teaching hungry souls to pray for the dead and for those souls who pray to the dead? There are no human beings on this planet that have been given the authority to alter the Word of God.

I see a very clear option before each of us. Do we want to live the life of a **Son of God** and live forever, or do we want to live the life of a **Son of Man** and life forever? I shall by the grace of God always choose to live my life as a **Son of God**.

No one ever invited me to an Apostolic Church, yet one day I found myself answering an invitation from the Lord Himself. I was on my way to mass one Sunday morning. I was going to St. Thomas Aquinas Roman Catholic Church when it seems in a moment in time I found myself sitting on the back pew of an Apostolic Church. The Lord by His Spirit led me to His house. I did not know exactly what I was doing there or exactly what I was looking for, but felt that I was there by Divine intervention.

I had barely gone inside when I noticed that there were no statues, only to learn later that God does not want statues in His House. He wants real live people worshipping Him in the Spirit and in Truth.

The second thing that I noticed was that there was no altar on the platform. I believed in transubstantiation, where the wafer is changed to the body and the wine to the blood of Christ. The Sacrament of the Eucharist.

Being aware of the insecurities and instability that religion had to offer, trying not to be melodramatic, I wholeheartedly looked through this unique window of opportunity.

I remember the first song that the saints of God sang that Sunday morning was "Jesus is coming down the road." Although I could not completely comprehend what was going on around me, the words of that beautiful song were sending me a very clear message. The song goes:

> "He will save and He will heal
> Just believe Him and He will
> Jesus is coming down the road."

The Lord not only gave me perfect direction to His house but personally led me down the road until I stood in front of the door that led to the sanctuary. A place of refuge from a very dark spiritual storm. I could feel a battle raging within. There was an evil spirit that was refusing to let go.

However, the excitement of literally knowing God engulfed my soul as I stood hurriedly trying to interpret with sensitity and accuracy the enticing Spirit that I was feeling. For the first time in my life, I was privileged to feel with the saints of God the Shekinah glory of the Lord. As I stood in wonderment of His Spirit, I knew that I had been watched over by the source of all life.

I often think of the words written by the Oneness minister G.T. Haywood:

> "I see a crimson stream of blood,
> It flows from Calvary,
> Its waves which reach the throne of God
> Are sweeping over me."

I watched as the saints of God lifted their hands toward heaven in effortless grace. I was not praying my rosary or talking to some medieval saint. I simply asked God if He could make it where I could lift my hands the way they did. I wanted to be a "Son of God."

That Sunday morning, I was not looking for entertainment. I was looking for a touch from the Master's hand. When the saints clapped their hands, it was unto the Lord and unto the Lord only.

I quickly learned that the house of God was not a theatre, the saints were not entertainers, and the setting was not that of Hollywood. I understand that to please the Lord there must be a disconnect from the entertainment industry that continually reaches out to the **Sons of Man** in the world as well as those individuals in *man-made* religious Christianity.

I felt my eyes blur with tears and then overflow. Standing alone yet not alone, I wept as I inadequately stood before Him. This had to be the most sensational experience of my life as I watched light confront the unfathomed depths of darkness.

This is exactly what *man-made* religious Christianity that is being led by the **Sons of Man** was trying desperately to keep me from. Could I be experiencing the New Birth? Oh, yes! I was!

I had tried diligently with sincerity and intellect to serve God with all that I had been taught. I did not know it during those years of my life, but I was trying to serve a Holy God as a **Son of Man** and not as a **Son of God**. On that special Sunday morning, the redeemed of the Lord would lovingly and carefully introduce to me the living Rose of Sharon. When I woke up that Sunday morning, I had absolutely no idea that I would personally come in contact with the Lily of the Valley.

A minister came to where I was standing among total strangers. Not knowing who I was or where I had come from, the man asked me if I wanted to go to the altar. I agreed. It apparently was obvious that I was being touched by those who prayed around me.

We do not need to quickly get people in the water of baptism because there is also a cleansing process that must take place at the altar. There is a real joy in repentance that must be the first step towards salvation.

The man of God asked me to kneel on the floor at their altar. When my knees touched the floor I realized that I was not kneeling in a confessional box in front of a mortal priest, but that I was literally kneeling in front of the High Priest the King of all Kings and the Lord of all of the Lords.

I repented before God, and I believe He forgave me of my sins. I would learn that He and He alone can forgive sins. They then told me that I needed to be re-baptized in Jesus' Name. I asked why in Jesus' Name. Those wonderful people were quick with their answers.

> "Neither is there salvation in any other: for there is none other name under heaven given among men, whereby we must be saved."

> Acts 4:12

I was quick to be baptized in Jesus' Name and all of a sudden here comes the promise. As I lifted my hands in praise unto Him, He filled me with the Holy Ghost. I spoke in other tongues as His Spirit gave utterance on that very special day in my life.

It seemed that Satan literally went out of the back door. I walked into that church building as a **Son of Man** not having the promise and walked out of that same building as a **Son of God** with the promise!

> "But the hour cometh, and now is, when the true worshippers shall worship the Father in Spirit and in Truth: for the Father seeketh such to worship him. God is a Spirit: and they that worship him MUST worship him in Spirit and in Truth."

> John 4:23-24

103

I have been walking in Beulah land now for forty-three years and can honestly say that I have never looked back to *man-made* religious Christianity that is being led by the **Sons of Man**.

God has not changed, and no, the gates of hell have NOT prevailed against His blood-washed church! There is a universal feeling among God's people that the dark clouds of the midnight hour are upon us. As the **Sons of God** we must continue to be more faithful to the truth of the Word of the Lord than the **Sons of Men** professing Christianity are faithful to their ritualisms and formalities.

It is still His Church. It is still His doctrine and the church is still being led by the **Sons of God** that have experienced for themselves the New Birth as was clearly outlined on the day of Pentecost almost two thousand years ago.

At that old-fashioned altar I received everything that I needed to live a victorious life and the power not only to keep me happy here below, but the authority to take me home when this life is over.

The End

CPSIA information can be obtained
at www.ICGtesting.com
Printed in the USA
FFOW05n0325300816

9 781628 800951